A New True Book

YOUR SKELETON AND SKIN

By Ray Broekel

This "true book" was prepared under the direction of
William H. Wehrmacher, M.D. FACC, FACP
Clinical Professor of Medicine and
Adjunct Professor of Physiology,
Loyola University Stritch School of Medicine, Chicago, Illinois,
with the help of his granddaughter Cheryl Sabey

CHILDRENS PRESS™

CHICAGO

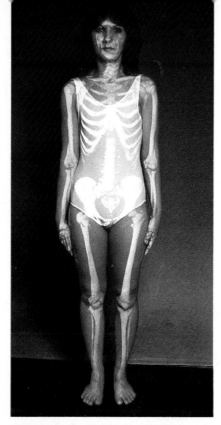

Photo of skeleton projected
on a human

PHOTO CREDITS

© L. V. Bergman & Associates, Inc.—Cover, 2, 4 (right), 7
(3 photos), 9 (2 photos), 21 (right), 23 (right), 25 (left), 28
(right), 29 (2 photos), 31 (left), 33 (3 photos), 34 (2 photos,
top, bottom left), 37 (right)

Field Museum of Natural History—4 (2 photos, left)

© Tony Freeman—5 (2 photos), 18 (3 photos), 39 (right), 45

© EKM-Nepenthe, photo by Tom Ballard—31 (right), 39
(left), 40, 42, 44

© Science Photo Library International, photo by Martin M.
Rotker—34 (bottom right)

© Denoyer-Geppert Co.—14

Drawings on pages 10, 13, 16, 17, 20, 21 (left, middle), 23
(left), 25 (right), 27, 28 (left), 33 (right), 37 (left) by Len
Meents

Library of Congress Cataloging in Publication Data

Broekel, Ray.
    Your skeleton and skin.

    (A New true book)
    Includes index.
    Summary: An introduction to each part of the
skeletal system and of the skin, using photographs
and drawings to depict details.
    1. Skeleton—Juvenile literature. 2. Skin—
Juvenile literature. [1. Skeleton. 2. Skin]
I. Title.
QM101.B85 1984   611'.7   84-7746
ISBN 0-516-01934-1   AACR2

TABLE OF CONTENTS

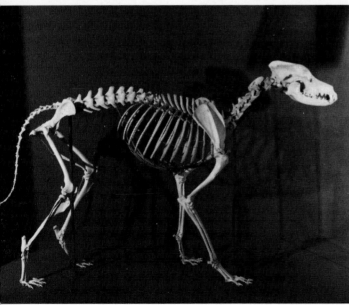

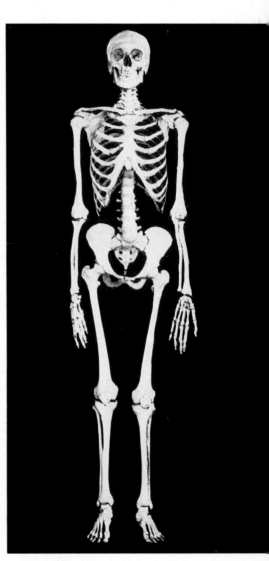

Skeletons of three gorillas (top left), domestic dog (bottom left), and a human. The adult human has 206 bones.

YOUR SKELETON

Your skeleton holds you
up. Your skin holds you in.

Humans have skeletons.
So do many kinds of
animals.

A human skeleton is
made up of bones. A baby
has about 350 bones in its

body. As the baby grows, some of those bones fuse, or join together.

By the time the baby becomes an adult its skeleton has 206 bones. The bones in a human form what is called the skeletal system.

The bones of the skeletal system have different jobs. Some bones protect other parts of the body. The skull bones protect the brain.

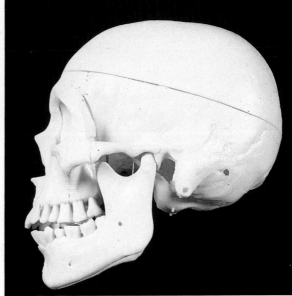

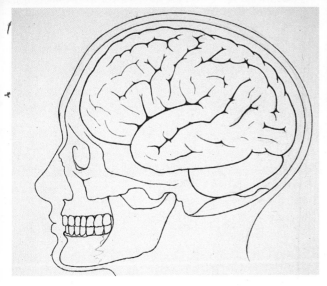

Skull bones (above) protect
the brain (bottom left)
from harm. The bones in
fingers and the wrist
allow these parts to move.

Some bones work
together to make different
body parts move. Hand
bones work together to
make fingers move.

7

BONES

Bones contain both living and nonliving things. Minerals are the main nonliving things. These minerals help make bones hard and strong.

The outer part of a bone is the hardest part. The inner part is called spongy bone. It has spaces

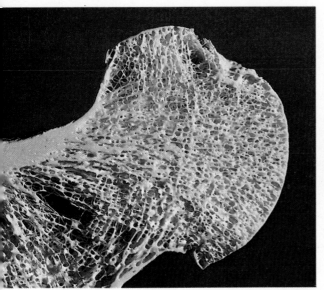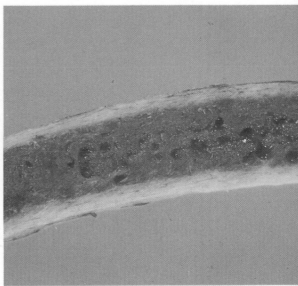

Inside of the femur, or thigh bone, (above left) shows the spongy bone.
The photograph at right shows human bone marrow.

between the bone matter.
Spongy bone is strong, but
not as hard as outer bone.
  At the center of many
bones is matter called
marrow. Red blood cells
are made in this marrow.

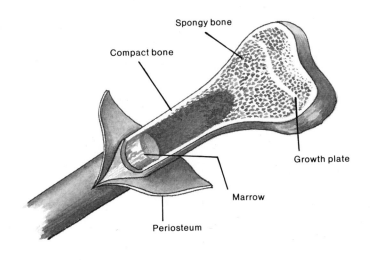

Spongy bone

Compact bone

Growth plate

Marrow

Periosteum

A thin layer called the periosteum covers bones except at the joints. The periosteum has living cells in it. These cells help bones grow. They also help repair bones when they are broken.

LIGAMENTS AND TENDONS

Ligaments hold the bones together in a living skeleton.

Ligaments are made of tough, living matter. Some ligaments are round. Other ligaments are flat. They look like ribbons or sheets of white, tough material.

Tendons are cords that connect muscles to bone.

JOINTS AND CARTILAGE

The places where bones come together are called joints. Some joints can move. There are movable joints in the backbone and in the elbow.

Between movable joints is found matter called cartilage. It is somewhat

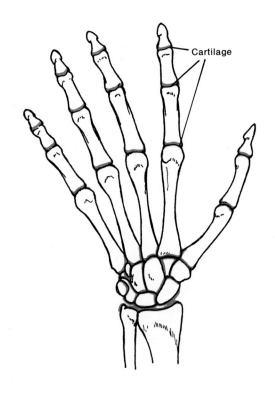

Cartilage

like a pad. A cartilage pad
forms a cushion between
bones as they come
together. Cartilage pads
the joints so they move
without pain.

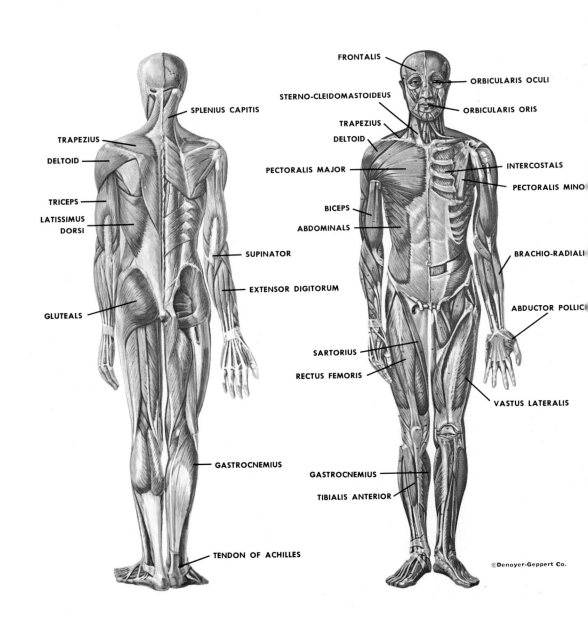

SPLENIUS CAPITIS

TRAPEZIUS

DELTOID

TRICEPS

LATISSIMUS DORSI

GLUTEALS

SUPINATOR

EXTENSOR DIGITORUM

GASTROCNEMIUS

TENDON OF ACHILLES

FRONTALIS

ORBICULARIS OCULI

STERNO-CLEIDOMASTOIDEUS

ORBICULARIS ORIS

TRAPEZIUS

DELTOID

PECTORALIS MAJOR

INTERCOSTALS

PECTORALIS MINO

BICEPS

ABDOMINALS

BRACHIO-RADIALI

ABDUCTOR POLLIC

SARTORIUS

RECTUS FEMORIS

VASTUS LATERALIS

GASTROCNEMIUS

TIBIALIS ANTERIOR

©Denoyer-Geppert Co.

MUSCLES

Living things move about. They can do this because of special cells called muscles that work together. A human has over six hundred muscles. Most are found in the arms and legs.

Many of the muscles in the body are called

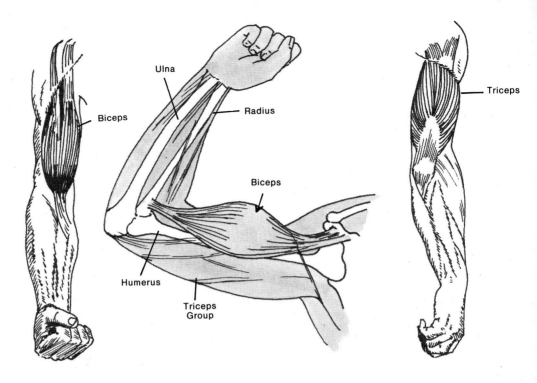

Biceps

Ulna

Radius

Biceps

Triceps

Humerus

Triceps
Group

skeletal muscles. These
muscles move the body
when we decide to move
the muscles.

Each skeletal muscle is
attached to two other parts
of the body. A muscle may
go from one bone to

another bone. Or it may go
from a bone to the skin.
Or a muscle may attach to
a tendon connected to a
bone.

One such tendon
connects a muscle in the
foot to the heel bone. It is
called the Achilles tendon
or heel cord.

Achilles tendon

Young people have thirty-three bones in their backbones. Some will grow together. Adults have twenty-six bones in their backbones.

THE BACKBONE

The backbone is also called the spine. Because of your backbone you can hold your upper body straight when you sit, stand, and walk.

The bones that make up the backbone are called vertebrae. The backbone of a child has thirty-three vertebrae. Some will grow together as the child grows older. Adults have only twenty-six vertebrae.

The vertebrae fit one on top of the other to form the backbone. A hole runs through each of the vertebrae to make the spinal canal. The spinal canal protects the spinal cord inside it.

There is cartilage between each of the

Right: Top view of a vertebra showing hole (neural canal) through which the spinal cord runs. Far right: Side view of a vertebra.

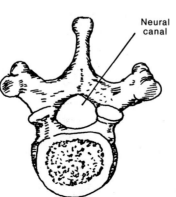

Neural canal

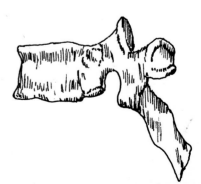

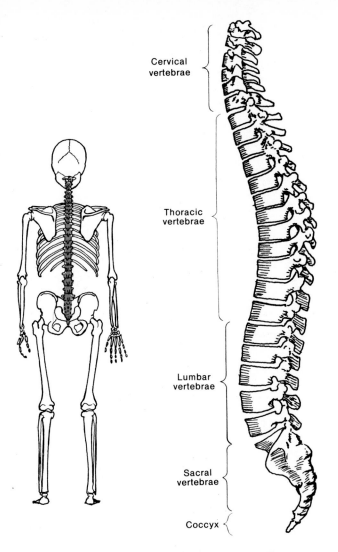

Cervical
vertebrae

Thoracic
vertebrae

Lumbar
vertebrae

Sacral
vertebrae

Coccyx

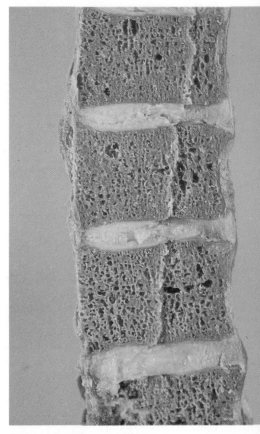

Spine showing cartilage

vertebrae. The cartilage
helps cushion the
vertebrae when they move
against each other.

THE HEAD BONES

The head bones, or skull, sit on top of the backbone. There are twenty-two bones in the skull. These bones fit together tightly.

The skull protects the brain. It also protects the eyes, nose, ears, and tongue. Teeth are attached to the skull and the jawbone.

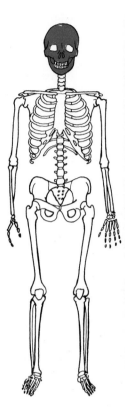

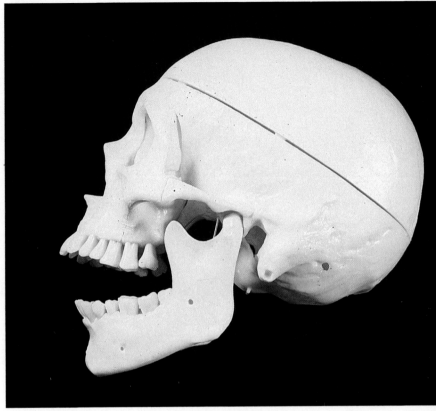

In the human skull the only bone
that moves is the jawbone.

Only one skull bone
moves. It is the bone that
allows you to eat and talk.
It is called the jawbone.

THE RIB CAGE

Ribs are bones that connect to other bones to form the rib cage. The rib cage protects the heart and lungs.

At the back of the rib cage the twelve pairs of ribs are connected to the backbone.

At the front, the top ten pairs of ribs are connected to a flat bone called the

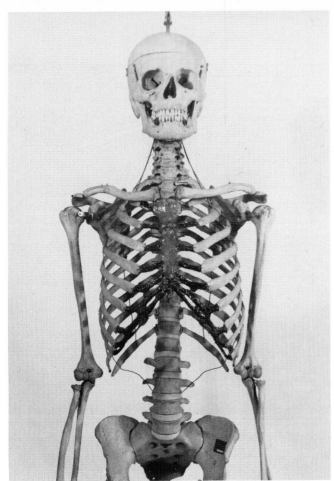

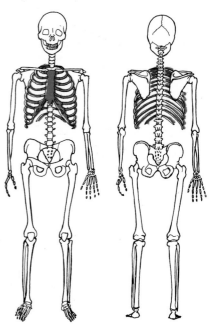

The rib cage protects the heart and lungs.

breastbone. The bottom
two pairs of ribs at the
front are connected only to
the backbone. So they are
called floating ribs.

COLLARBONES, SHOULDER BLADES, AND ARMS

There are two collarbones. One end of each is connected to the breastbone. The other end is connected to the arm socket of the shoulder blade. The collarbones and shoulder blades form something like crossbars. The arms hang from these crossbars.

The long, thick bone in the upper arm is called

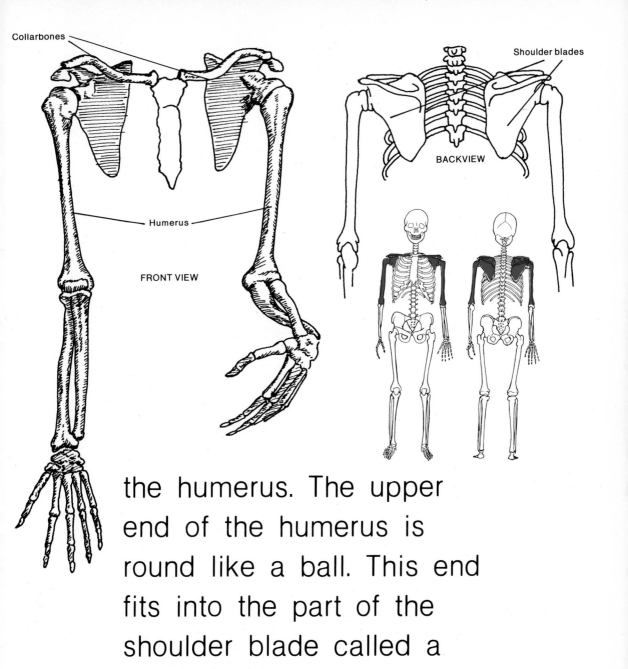

Collarbones

Humerus

FRONT VIEW

Shoulder blades

BACKVIEW

the humerus. The upper
end of the humerus is
round like a ball. This end
fits into the part of the
shoulder blade called a
socket. This ball-shaped

27

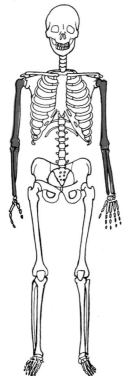

Ball-and-socket
joint at shoulder

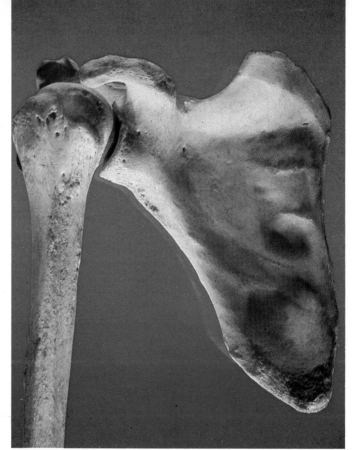

end can move freely in the shoulder socket. It is a ball-and-socket joint.

The upper arm is connected to two bones in the lower arm. They are

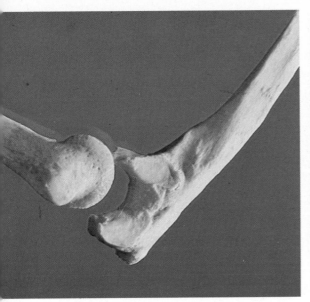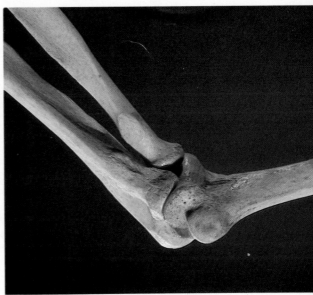

Two views of the hinge joint at the elbow

the ulna and the radius.
Those three bones, the
humerus, ulna, and radius,
are connected at the
elbow.

That connection is called
a hinge joint. At a hinge
joint only back and forth
movement can be made.

WRISTBONES AND HAND BONES

The arm bones are connected to the wristbones. There are eight wristbones. They are called carpals. To them are connected the five metacarpal bones. And finally come the finger bones. Each finger has three. They are called phalanges.

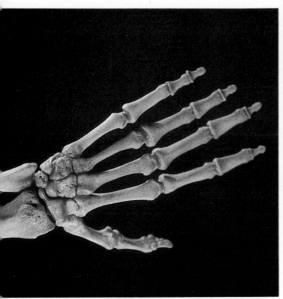

View of hand and wrist bones (left).
These bones allow movement.
Humans have thumbs that work against
the fingers to hold and grip things.

The thumb has only two
phalanges. A human thumb
moves about freely. The
thumb works against the
fingers so that things can
be grasped and picked up
easily.

HIP BONES AND LEG BONES

The thigh bone, or femur, is the largest bone in the skeleton. The femur connects to the hip bone in a ball-and-socket joint like the shoulder joint.

The hip bones are part of the pelvis. The pelvis protects the organs inside the lower body.

Connected to each leg bone at the knee are two bones, the fibula and the tibia. The knee is a hinge joint like the elbow. It can move back and forth,

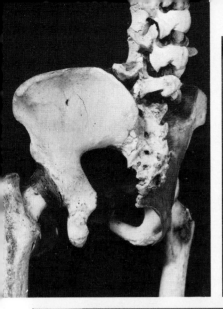

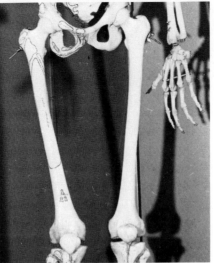

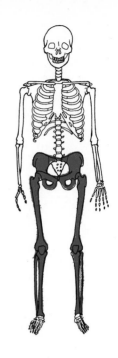

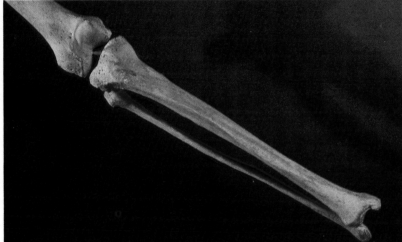

Top right: Pelvis, hip,
and thigh
bones
Top left: Close-up of
the hip bone
Left: Knee bone,
fibula, and tibia

but not from side to
side. The knee cap, or
patella, protects the ends
of the bones at the joint.

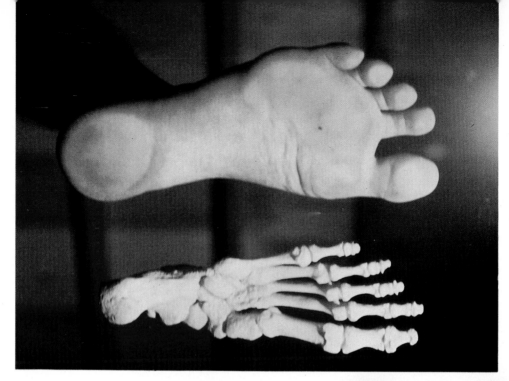

Human foot and skeleton (above), X-ray of foot (bottom right), and photograph showing how foot bones work together to allow movement (bottom left)

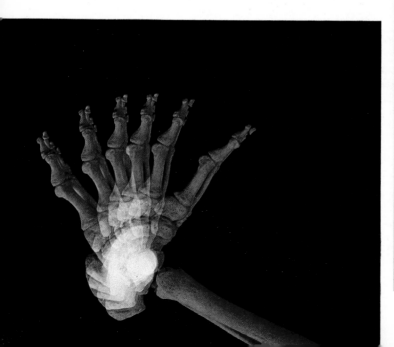

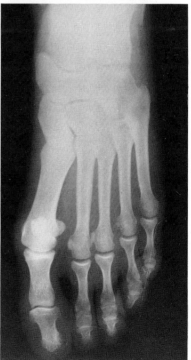

FOOT BONES

The ankles are the lower part of the two leg bones, the fibula and tibia.

The heel and six other bones called the tarsals form the back of the foot. Five metatarsal bones in the middle of the foot connect the tarsals with the short bones in the toes called phalanges, just as the short bones in the fingers are called phalanges.

THE SKIN

Skin is the body's outer protective cover. Human skin does many jobs. It is almost waterproof. It keeps water from entering the body. It keeps body liquids from leaking out unless there is need for them to leave. Sweat is a body liquid.

Skin stretches with the movements of the body. And skin helps to control body heat.

Skin is made of several

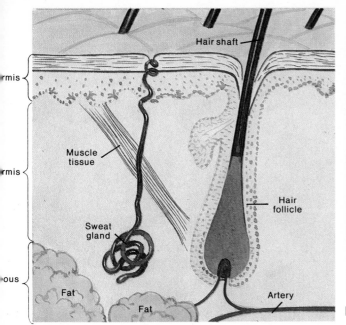

Hair shaft

Muscle tissue

Sweat gland

Fat

Fat

Hair follicle

Artery

rmis

rmis

ous

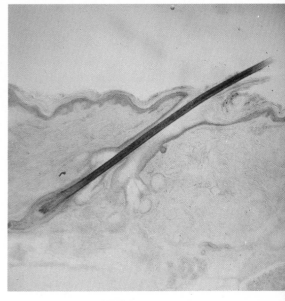

Human hair magnified ten times

layers. The outer layer is the epidermis, and it also has several layers.

The outside of the epidermis is tough and transparent. The cells at this layer are dead or dying. As these dead cells fall off, new cells from a layer just underneath replace them.

Through the transparent layer of epidermis can be seen the color in the next layer. That layer contains pigment. And pigment gives color to skin.

In the outer epidermis are small openings called pores. Sweat is given off through some of them. Hair grows through others.

Sweat glands are found in the dermis layer of the

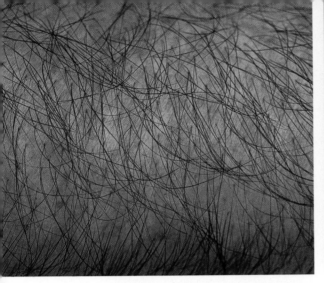

skin, throughout the body.
The insides of your hands
and the bottoms of your
feet have the most sweat
glands.

When your body is hot,
the pores open. Then sweat
is given off. The pores are
closed at other times.

Hair roots, called follicles,
are found in the dermis.

Oil glands throughout your body help lubricate the skin and hair. This oil often collects on your nose. Rub your nose as a test.

Oil glands come up next to the hair roots. The oil keeps the skin from drying out and cracking.

Oil glands are found over most of your body. But there are none on the inside of the hands and the bottoms of the feet.

SENSE ORGANS

Your skin has five kinds
of sense organs in it.
These sense organs react
to heat, cold, pain,
pressure, and touch by
sending messages to the
brain.

If you touch something
hot, heat sense organs
react. Messages are

The heat sense organs in this man's body reacted when he touched the hot cookie sheet with bare hands.

quickly sent to the brain.
You pull your hand back.
  If you stick your hand in ice
water, the cold sense organs
in your skin send messages
to your brain and you will
pull your hand back.

FINGERPRINTS AND FOOTPRINTS

Skin on the inside of your hands and on the bottom of your feet is different from skin on other parts of the body. The skin in these places has raised lines called ridges.

Look at the ridges on your fingertips. The ridges form a pattern, or design. Prints can be made of these ridge patterns. They are called fingerprints.

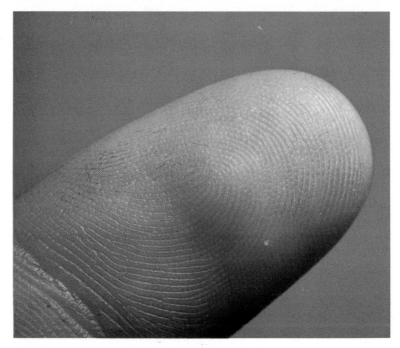
Close-up of the ridges on a finger

No one else in the world has the same ridge patterns as you. And no two people in the world have the same fingerprints. So fingerprints can be used to identify people.

HURRAH FOR SKIN AND SKELETON

Your skin holds you in
from head to toe.
Your skeleton holds you up
when you sit or go.

Without the two
what might you be?
A bunch of stuff
just running free.

WORDS YOU SHOULD KNOW

SKELETON

Achilles tendon(ah • KIL • eez TEN • dun)—the heel cord; named after a story about the Greek warrior Achilles who could only be injured in the heel cord

ball-and-socket joint(BALL AND SOCK • et JOYNT)—bone connection at which there is free movement

bone(BOAN)—hard piece of matter that forms the skeleton

cartilage(CAR • tih • ledj)—matter that serves as a cushion between bones

femur(FEE • mer)—largest bone in the human skeleton, a leg bone

hinge joint(HINJ JOYNT)—bone connection at which only back and forth movement can be made

joint(JOYNT)—place where two or more parts come together

ligaments(LIG • ah • ments)—tough living matter that hold bones together

lubricate(LOO • brih • kait)—to make smooth and slippery

marrow(MAIR • oh)—matter found at the center of many bones; place where red blood cells are made

minerals(MIN • er • els)—nonliving matter that helps make bones hard and strong

muscle(MUSS • ill)—group of special cells used to make body parts move

patella(pah • TEL • ah)—kneecap which protects bones at the knee joint

periosteum(pair • ee • AHSS • tee • um)—thin layer, containing living cells, covering bones except at joints

phalanges(fay • LANJ • ez)—short bones found in fingers and toes

rib cage(RIB KAIJ)—collection of bones that protects the heart and lungs

skeleton(SKEL • ih • tun)—a supporting bony framework for a body

skull(SKUL)—the head bone, made of twenty-two bones that fit tightly together

spongy bone(SPUNJ • ee BOAN)—has more spaces between bone matter than does outer bone

system(SIS • tem) — a group of parts or things that are so related or that act together in such a way that they are considered as a whole — such as a skeletal system

tendon(TEN • dun) — body part that connects a muscle to a bone

thumb(THUM) — the short, thick finger nearest the wrist

vertebrae(VER • tih • bray) — bones that form the backbone, or spine

SKIN

cell(SEL) — the tiny basic unit of all living matter

dermis(DER • miss) — the layer of skin beneath the epidermis

epidermis(EP • ih • der •miss) — outer layer of the skin

fingerprint(FING • er • print) — an impression of the ridge pattern on the inner side at the tip of a finger

follicle(FOL • ih • kil) — a sac in the body in which hair roots grow

gland(GLAND) — an organ that produces and stores or gives off certain substances

organ(OR • gen) — any part of a body that has a special job; heat sense organs react to heat

pattern(PAT • tern) — an arrangement of markings

pigment(PIG • ment) — a natural substance that colors living cells

pore(POAR) — a tiny opening in the skin

pressure(PRESH • er) — the state of being pressed

ridge(RIJ) — a raised line or strip

skin(SKIN) — outer part of the body which protects the inner part

sweat(SWET) — the salty moisture given off through the pores of the skin

INDEX

About the Author

Ray Broekel is well known in the publishing field as a teacher, editor, and author of science materials for young people. A full-time freelance writer, Dr. Broekel also writes many other kinds of books for both young people and adults. He has had over 150 published. His first book was published by Childrens Press in 1956. Ray Broekel lives with his wife, Peg, and a dog, Fergus, in Ipswich, Massachusetts.